TAKING THE FRUIT

Modern Women's
Tales of the Bible

A beautiful storybook. Come here, dear women and men, and examine this lovely storybook which, since the world has existed, has never appeared in print. With twenty-three stories, all of which are made out of the Torah, and some also from the Talmud, you should read this book and enjoy!

WOMAN'S INSTITUTE FOR CONTINUING JEWISH EDUCATION
SAN DIEGO

On the preceding page is our modern version of a dedication originally found in the *Ma'aseh Book,* Basle, 1602. For the original, please see Chava Weissler reference in "Sources."

Library of Congress Card Number: 88-51162
ISBN 0-9608054-8-6

TAKING THE FRUIT

Modern Women's
Tales of the Bible

Jane Sprague Zones, Editor

Contents

Preface to the New Edition

"Midrashic process" works! This was the term first used in the 1981 introduction to *Taking the Fruit: Modern Women's Tales of the Bible,* a collection of modern midrashim gathered from classroom writings at the Woman's Institute for Continuing Jewish Education in San Diego.

In that introduction, midrashic process was described as the steps women could take to create a midrash. As a result of this "ground-breaking" instruction (according to Sue Levi Elwell in *The Jewish Women's Studies Guide, Second Edition*), teachers and study groups across the country adopted the process for teaching the modern midrash. Consequently, the proliferation of midrashim has been so great that writer Aviva Cantor declared in her introduction to *The Jewish Woman: A Bibliography, 1900-1985,* that midrash writing in the United States has burgeoned into "a cottage industry."

What is most exciting for us as educators is to observe not only the involvement of women in the external midrashic process (the writing of midrashim), but also in the internal process of learning and growing that occurs when people begin to create. Watching women grow in self-esteem and achievement as they master this historical Jewish craft provides us with a profound sense of wonder and accomplishment. This is Jewish education at its best.

Because of the number of new and innovative midrashim, the Woman's Institute For Continuing Jewish Education invited women nationwide to submit their works for our new edition. This book now contains not only early midrashim from San Diego, but also later ones from other parts of the United States and from Israel. In common, these midrashim demonstrate women's need to scrutinize the text and bring it into their lives with their own understanding of history. It is for most a labor of love—their personal affair with the Torah.

Irene Fine

Prologue

When the woman saw that the tree was good for eating and a delight to the eyes, and that the tree was desirable as a source of wisdom, she took of its fruit and ate. (Genesis 3:6)

What was the wisdom learned in the garden?

In the beginning the women told their stories. Sitting in the garden at twilight, under the tree of knowledge, they spun and wove tales about the courageous deeds of their foremothers. With flames of imagination igniting their souls, they sat before the fire and shared the glorious deeds that had been their spiritual inheritance. The miracle of the garden was that each and every woman added her part so that the generations were not separate from each other but instead were joined by common experiences and a shared history.

Over time they were forced to leave the idyllic existence of the garden. Wandering far away, the women searched for work to support themselves and their families. No longer did they have time to tell the stories which kept their myths alive, for now their labor was great, their tasks arduous. Their first responsibility was to their family, to put food on the table. They thought it was more important that their husbands should study than that they should tell stories. If the men didn't study, the law would be forgotten. If the law was forgotten, all would be chaos. So the women labored on, always the helpmates so that others would survive. During moments of rest, when people gathered for pleasure, the women no longer heard their names mentioned in the stories that were told. They thought it odd that no one noticed their work. Still, they labored on. Soon, however, they began to feel estranged from each other and wondered why. Eventually their work lost meaning, and they drifted in their thoughts, sometimes in their actions.

One day quite by accident, the garden wall was rediscovered. It was long and high and looked as though it could not be breached. But several women struggling together found a way over the wall, and once on the other side, they discovered a path which led them back to the tree of knowledge. In their joy and excitement, they told others. Soon, more women found their way to the garden.

One night, when several had gathered together under the tree, one woman stood up and became a storyteller for the rest. She began by recalling the deeds of her mother and her mother's mother. In due time she even remembered events which took her back to the original experience in the garden. At first, while she was telling her story, the others pulled down inside themselves and huddled closer to the ground, lest they be called upon to recite. "It's been so long," they thought, "how will we remember? Aren't we supposed to tell things exactly as they happened?" But the words of the storyteller were clear and sweet. And as she gathered strength, so did the others.

Soon they were all adding bits and pieces to the stories, which eventually became treasured histories, precious myths, and sacred truths. When the original accounts were no longer remembered, they made them up, captured by the spirit of invention. As the evening went on, the women realized they had recovered the power of storytelling and in so doing had also uncovered the source of their own vitality. Thus their experiences began to have shape, purpose, destiny. For the first time since the expulsion, the women moved closer to each other, no longer strangers.

At dawn, the women slowly stood up and prepared for their work outside the garden. Although they were reluctant to leave, they knew instinctively they would return, for now they understood the importance of their gathering. Through the experience of storytelling, they had regained knowledge of their singular inheritance, and in the process had prepared a magnificent legacy for all who would come after them. The experience in the garden was only a beginning.

Irene Fine

Introduction:
Begetting a Midrash

The story you have just read is a midrash. It is an exposition of a biblical theme which concerns the Garden of Eden and what happened there. It is also a modern story that attempts to reflect the feelings, hopes, and aspirations of contemporary women which were not written about in the biblical text.

The classic definition of a midrash is a short explanation of a biblical passage. Two types of midrashim (plural) exist: one is halachic, and concerned primarily with law; the other is aggadic, and concerned mainly with non-legal issues.

The tradition of creating midrash is an ancient one. When Ezra the Scribe returned from Babylonian captivity, he proclaimed a public reading of the law in order to make the teachings of the Torah meaningful to a new generation. Nehemiah 8:8 relates: "And they [the scribes] read in the book, in the Law of God, distinctly; and they gave the sense, and caused them to understand the reading." In other words, in order to make the Torah understandable, Ezra and the scribes interpreted the Torah or "gave the sense." Thus they created midrash, orally at first.

The people must have loved hearing the fresh new interpretations of biblical themes, because since that time, midrash has become one of the most important mediums of Jewish expression. Much of the source material for midrashic stories originated with the common people. Fanciful ideas and colorful outpourings were brought into the academies by the rabbis when they could be used to explicate a text. Legends, sayings, and folklore were reworked, given the rabbinic stamp of approval, and eventually these imaginative stories wove themselves into the fabric of Jewish life. Centuries later when scholars studied Jewish history, they had difficulty distinguishing the actual from the fabrication in Jewish storytelling.

Midrash has always served an important function in Jewish life. The stories keep alive biblical themes. They teach us our history in a remarkably simple and memorable way. Most importantly, the stories build a bridge between past and present so that each new generation of Jews is linked to the preceding one; each succeeding generation can define itself in terms of the biblical text. By creating and telling these stories, a relationship with Torah is maintained and kept alive over the centuries.

It was for this reason that the Woman's Institute For Continuing Jewish Education first collected stories and published this book. One way for women to relieve the tension created in a relationship between the static written Torah and the modern changing world is for each generation to read the text with fresh and open eyes. Women's roles in the Torah were circumscribed and limited while women's roles in the modern world are expanding. Therefore, it is incumbent upon contemporary women to study the text and to write modern stories that maintain a relationship with the text, incorporating their own experiences and consciousness into Judaism. This midrashic process allows Judaism to grow and develop a healthy relationship with all of its people.

What is the midrashic process? Three steps are involved. The first step is to read the biblical text. For instance, there are two versions of how the first woman was created. The better known version is the one in which Eve is formed from Adam's rib (Genesis 2:21-22). There is, however, an earlier version found in Genesis 1:27: "And God created man in His image, in the image of God He created him; male and female He created them."

As the reader will note, the text is very brief; it does not give much information or elaborate on the given theme. The text simply states what the situation is. It is left for later generations to give shape to the unexpressed.

The second step is to read the post-biblical midrashim and see how later generations explained the biblical passage to their contemporaries. (Selected sources are listed on page 99.) For instance, the following midrash was written by the rabbis to explain who that first woman was who was created before Eve:

> The divine resolution to bestow a companion on Adam met the wishes of man, who had been overcome by a feeling of isolation when the animals came to him in pairs to be named. To banish his loneliness, Lilith was first given to Adam as his wife. Like him, she had been created out of the dust of the ground. But she remained with him only a short time, because she insisted upon enjoying full equality with her husband.
>
> She derived her rights from their identical origin. With the help of the Ineffable Name, which she pronounced, Lilith flew away from Adam, and vanished in the air. Adam complained before God that the wife He had given him had deserted him, and God sent forth three angels to

capture her. They found her in the Red Sea, and they sought to make her go back with the threat that, unless she went, she would lose a hundred of her demon children daily by death. But Lilith preferred this punishment to living with Adam. She takes her revenge by injuring babes—baby boys during the first night of their life, while baby girls are exposed to her wicked designs until they are twenty days old. The only way to ward off the evil is to attach an amulet bearing the names of her three angel captors to the children, for such had been the agreement between them.

(Ginzberg, Vol. I, pp. 65-66)

The third and last step is to explain the biblical passage in light of women's experience today. This time, after rereading the biblical passage, the midrash writer (in order to explain the text further) asks a question of the text. Her answer is the midrash. Examples of contemporary midrashim related to the traditional one above are found on pages 15, 23, and 27.

Through the act of creation, women today can define themselves and their ability in positive terms rather than negative ones, and thus can take a strong, realistic, and equal role in Jewish history. This is the power of midrash. In earlier midrashim, ones in which women were written about by men, negative images abound. For example, again starting with the biblical text in Genesis 19:26, Lot's wife is mentioned, but the text does not name or tell us anything about this woman, let alone explain reasons for her actions.

"Lot's wife looked back, and she turned into a pillar of salt." (Genesis 19:26)

In later rabbinic midrash her behavior is explained in clearly negative terms. She is portrayed as a gossip who betrays the presence of two angels who have entered Lot's home.

> Lot divided his dwelling in two parts, one for himself and his guests, the other for his wife, so that, if aught happened, his wife would be spared. Nevertheless it was she who betrayed him. She went to a neighbor and borrowed some salt, and to the question, whether she could not have supplied herself with salt during daylight hours, she replied, "We had enough salt, until some guests came to us; for them we needed more."
>
> (Ginzberg, Vol. I, p. 254)

In our time female images have been transformed. In the midrashim on pp. 37 and 41, Lot's wife is reflected in a new light, in a much more compassionate manner. In one of these midrashim, in fact, Lot's wife is identified and named, and her name, Tova ("good"), reflects her new positive identity.

Midrash can be used in many ways, and the adventurous will devise ways to incorporate these stories into their Jewish lives. Midrash, for example, can be used in holiday or festival celebrations where life-affirming images of women are needed. B'not Mitzvah, Midlife or Wise Woman ceremonies, and Rosh Hodesh celebrations come immediately to mind. Midrash can be used in consciousness-raising situations or in classrooms when complicated human behavior cannot easily be explained in a more direct fashion. The only limit to the use of midrash is the imagination of the user...and we all know how inventive women are!

Every Jew has at least one midrash in her that needs to be written. It is our hope that you will connect with the text and become a part of Jewish history by engaging in the adventure of creating midrash. Read your favorite biblical passage, savor the text in the spirit in which it was written, and see whether the story strikes a responsive chord and awakens in you another story that you can write and share with others. Toward that end, we have reserved the final pages of this book for **Your Own Midrash**. And who knows? One midrash may beget another. If we all write our stories down, we will all profit from our shared experience.

Perhaps you have never written a midrash. We know the first one may be difficult. You will probably write as if generations of scholars were reading over your shoulder and criticizing your efforts. You may think, ''Who am I to be writing midrash?'' These negative thoughts are just a reflection of the negative images of women from the writings in the past. Here is your chance to help change the direction of storytelling for all women.

It might be helpful to think of yourself as the woman in the last midrash (page 97), cultivating a new field. Perhaps you, too, will hear a strong voice in your head, one that urges you to **"Do it!"** Then, sit down, take out a pen, and begin...''Let me tell you a story....''

Irene Fine

And God said, "Let us make man in our image, after our likeness." (Genesis 1:26)

What image did God have in mind when creating man?

After God created the heaven and the earth with all their accessories, She created a baby from the dust. The baby lived in the Garden of Eden, drinking milk, sleeping, and relieving himself. He cried out to God almost continuously, so unhappy was he with his role in life.

"Blessed Creator," he would sob. "What kind of life have You given me? All I can do is crawl in the dirt like a snake. Change me so I can overcome this frustration."

God listened to the baby's cries, feeling maternal stirrings in Her breast. So, She granted the baby's wish and made him into a toddler.

Soon he began to whine again. "Blessed Creator, You treat me unfairly. I have legs to walk, yet stumble and fall. I have words but no one understands their meaning. Change me so I can overcome these frustrations."

God heard the toddler's pleas and in Her motherly wisdom knew that he needed to grow. So, She granted the toddler's wish and made him into a little boy.

Soon the little boy began to pout. "Blessed Creator, I am bored. There is nothing in the garden to do. I am too small to work the land but too big to play in the sand. Give me a purpose in life so I can overcome these frustrations."

God accepted the little boy's need to be challenged and felt pride in his desire to become part of a larger whole. So, She granted the little boy's wish and made him into a teenager.

Soon the teenager began his angry protests. "Blessed Creator, how can You do this to me? I have a body but I barely know it. One day I turn around and I am dotted in pimples and new hair. And my voice is a disgrace—the animals laugh at me or are frightened away. I demand that You change me so I can overcome these frustrations."

God empathized with the teenager and shared in his discomfort. So, She granted the teenager's wish and made him into an adult.

Soon the adult began to lecture. "Blessed Creator, you have not given me adequate options. I must work too hard caring for the world You have created, and the responsibility is overwhelming. I am under too much stress and implore You to reconsider Your plan for me so I can overcome these frustrations."

God acknowledged the adult's anxiety and felt pangs of guilt for overburdening him. So, She granted the adult's wish and changed him into a middle-aged man.

Soon the middle-aged man began to complain. "Blessed Creator, I gave You my best and what have I to show for it? None of the prime jobs go to me anymore. I am treated like I am over the hill. No status, no respect, no sense of usefulness. I deserve more in life. Change me so I can overcome these frustrations."

God recognized the despair in the middle-aged man, and

She was saddened. So, She granted the middle-aged man's wish and changed him into an old man.

Soon the old man began to cry. "Blessed Creator, put an end to my misery. My bones are brittle, my teeth are gone, and my hair is falling away. I can barely see or hear and food is tasteless to me now. I have served You well and reached some goals. Spare me further pain and allow me to overcome these frustrations."

God felt mercy in Her being for She could not bear this old man's suffering. So, She granted the old man's wish and changed him into dust.

After closing the old man's eyes forever and taking the breath from his lips, God sat down in the Garden of Eden and cried because She was overcome with all these frustrations.

Randee Friedman

And God created man in His image, in the image of God He created him; male and female He created them. (Genesis 1:27)

As Rashi notes, the two stories of creation appear to be contradictory: "Male and female He created them" (Genesis 1:27), and further on "and He took one of his ribs and closed up the flesh at that spot." (Genesis 2:21)

Rashi cites a midrash in Erubin 18a: God created the human at first with two faces, and then later divided the human. . . . But Rashi prefers the explanation: "Here it tells you they were both created on the sixth day but it doesn't say how. Later it tells you how they were created."

Not until the eighth century CE do we find the famous midrash of Lilith's flight from the garden recorded in the *Alphabet of Ben Sirach,* although we may assume the version was orally transmitted some time before it was recorded. This version moves from the notion of a hermaphrodite, or two-faced creature, to the notion of an independent female created as an equal.

The intriguing question: Who was or were the authors of this midrashic leap into a new conception? It seems likely the authors were women.

The two midrash poems that follow, the first written in 1973 and the second in 1988, chart the evolution of Rabbi Lynn Gottlieb, the author, in relationship to Lilith's passion, fierce independence, and night wisdom.

First Tale (1973)

In the beginning
God made the earth and the sky and the sea
God reached into the waters
formed a womb in my hand
and put it in the sky
then
with Her own breath
God filled the womb with Lilith
first woman

Deep inside the womb
Lilith began her birthing
the womb grew heavy with woman
until one day
Lilith pushed her arms outward
tore the walls which held her
to reach the sky

The sky received her smiling
Lilith embraced all life
her wings of fire
not knowing where sky began
and her own self ended

Lilith looked down
saw a shadow on the water
She saw herself hovering over the deep
Lilith rejoiced
thinking she had found another like herself
spoke to the image
which did not answer
First loneliness

and God said: it is not good
for woman to be alone
I will make her a companion
as Lilith is sky
so man shall be earth
and God made man
from the dust of the ground
breathed into him the breath of life
and man became a living being

then God brought Lilith to dry land
there upon the soil
Lilith became still
seeing a place which did not move
like wind or water
Lilith said:
I will stay awhile

then, he appeared
and came toward her
his eyes still spoke of birth
like hers
and yet she knew a difference
this one stood solid on the ground

He said: I am Adam child of Adamah
walk with me and I will show you the earth
Lilith smiled and said: I am Lilith
with wings of fire
come and I will show you the sky
but Adam, afraid of Lilith's wings of fire
fell to the earth

Lilith
needing her companion
removed her wings of fire

hurled them to the sky
Adam saw Lilith without her fire
no longer afraid
he rose to meet her
woman and man walked together
sharing memories of their own first hours
Lilith remembered a spirit on the waters
called to the sun to return her fire
Adam knew her now
and would not be afraid

but Adam
still afraid of woman's fire
forced Lilith to the ground
hoping to make her
more like himself
but she continued calling
then Adam understood
the power of his holding
forced himself down upon her
Lilith felt his strength as pain
closed her eyes
first sleep of terror

deep inside her own darkness
under the fear of man
Lilith forgot her sky birth
and awoke
without memory

Eve
second woman
Eve opened her eyes
saw Adam standing large before her
he moved and revealed the sun

Adam said: I will call you woman
because you come from man
serve me
and I will protect you from strange fires

Eve upon the earth
gave herself to man
and God sad parent of creation
wept
seeing woman slave to man
and man afraid of woman
God knew
she must give them life and death
the passing of generations
so one future man and woman
could come together
as intended at creation

and God planted the tree of knowledge in the garden saying
You must choose eternity or knowledge
for on the day you eat this fruit
you shall surely die

and Eve said: I want to know
and felt a strange remembering
she saw the tree was good for food
and a delight to the eyes
so she took the fruit and ate it
Adam ate with her

then Eve heard the evening wind
moving in the garden
and some dark memory stirred her soul
a memory of fire
a spirit on the waters

Adam saw death
the lost eternity of man
and said: In pain you shall bear my children
your desire will be toward me
Eve left the garden
with her master
mourning a self not quite remembered

Lilith
we are your children
we are the changing generations
help us recover our wings of fire
so we can come together
woman and man
as intended by God
in the beginning
of creation

Lilith's Songs of Creation (1988)

Night wind
Screech owl
Harpie in the sea
Womanbody
Winged one
Hag in me
Soaked in oil
Till I slither like a snake
Hot with desire
For the worlds I create
Dog bitch
Long haired
Woman of the night
Howling heart of the moon
Fears take flight
The earth is born
In my dark body
In my dark body
The earth is born.

Rabbi Lynn Gottlieb

A midrash on Genesis chapters 1 - 3.

The author is doing midrash on midrash and is concerned with women's experience. Her question: How can I express the meaning of consciousness-raising in a Jewish context?

In the beginning, the Lord God formed Adam and Lilith from the dust of the ground and breathed into their nostrils the breath of life. Created from the same source, they were equal in all ways. Adam, being a man, didn't like this situation, and he looked for ways to change it. He said, "I'll have my figs now, Lilith," ordering her to wait on him, and he tried to leave to her the daily tasks of life in the garden. But Lilith wasn't one to take any nonsense; she picked herself up, uttered God's holy name, and flew away. "Well now, Lord," complained Adam, "that uppity woman you sent me has gone and deserted me." The Lord, inclined to be sympathetic, sent his messengers after Lilith, telling her to shape up and return to Adam or face dire punishment. She, however, preferring anything to living with Adam, decided to stay right where she was. And so God, after more careful consideration this time, caused a deep sleep to fall upon Adam and out of one of his ribs created for him a second companion, Eve.

For a time, Eve and Adam had quite a good thing going. Adam was happy now, and Eve, though she occasionally sensed capacities within herself which remained undeveloped, was basically satisfied with her role as Adam's wife and helper. The only thing that really disturbed her was the excluding closeness of the relationship between Adam and God. Adam and God just seemed to have more in common, both being men, and Adam came to identify with God more and more. After a while, that made God a bit uncomfortable, too, and he started going over in his mind whether he may not have made a mistake letting Adam talk him into banishing Lilith and creating Eve, seeing the power that gave Adam.

Meanwhile Lilith, all alone, attempted from time to time to rejoin the human community in the garden. After her first fruitless attempt to breach its walls, Adam worked hard to build them stronger, even getting Eve to help him. He told her fearsome stories of the demon Lilith who threatens women in childbirth and steals children from their cradles in the middle of the night. The second time Lilith came, she stormed the garden's main gate, and a great battle between her and Adam ensued in which she was finally defeated. This time, however, before Lilith got away, Eve got a glimpse of her and saw she was a woman like herself.

After this encounter, seeds of curiosity and doubt began to grow in Eve's mind. Was Lilith indeed just another woman? Adam had said she was a demon. Another woman! The very idea attracted Eve. She had never seen another creature like herself before. And how beautiful and strong Lilith had looked! How bravely she had fought! Slowly, slowly, Eve began to think about the limits of her own life within the garden.

One day, after many months of strange and disturbing thoughts, Eve, wandering around the edge of the garden, noticed a young apple tree she and Adam had planted and saw that one of its branches stretched over the garden wall. Spontaneously, she tried to climb it, and, struggling to the top, swung herself over the wall.

She did not wander long on the other side before she met the one she had come to find, for Lilith was waiting. At first sight of her, Eve remembered the tales of Adam and was frightened—but Lilith understood and greeted her kindly. "Who are you?" they asked each other. "What is your story?" And they sat and spoke together of the past and then of the future. They talked for many hours, not once, but many times. They taught each other many things, and told each other stories, and laughed together, and cried, over and over, till the bond of sisterhood grew between them.

Meanwhile, back in the garden, Adam was puzzled by Eve's comings and goings and disturbed by what he sensed to be her new attitude toward him. He talked to God about it, and God, having his own problems with Adam and a somewhat broader perspective, was able to help him out a little—but he was confused too. Something had failed to go according to plan. As in the days of Abraham, he needed counsel from his children. "I am who I am," thought God, "but I must become who I will become."

And God and Adam were expectant and afraid the day Eve and Lilith returned to the garden, bursting with possibilities, ready to rebuild it together.

Judith Plaskow

It is not good for man to be alone; I will make a fitting helper for him. (Genesis 2:18)

And who is this helper? How do we know her?

God created Adam and Lilith. Adam said to Lilith, "God created me first, therefore I have power and authority and strength; I am better than you." Lilith said to Adam, "God created me second. Through me He corrected His mistakes and created a more perfect being: more pleasing to the eye, sensitive to the world, and courageous enough to stand alone if I must."

Adam spent his days proving his superiority. He climbed the highest trees and found the most succulent fruit. And always he would return to Lilith and say, "You see, I am superior." And Lilith spent her days befriending the animals and exploring her new environment, experiencing the joy of each new encounter. At first Lilith would return to Adam and, with excitement, share her day's taste of life with him. "What you are doing is a waste of time," said Adam. "I, on the other hand, climbed the highest tree and looked out over all the world. I am better than you."

Soon Lilith kept quiet and did not share her day's taste of life with Adam. Lilith and Adam began to argue over silly things.

One day Adam said to Lilith, "You do not respect my authority; you must leave this place." One day Lilith said to Adam, "You criticize everything I say and do unless it is about you. I need to find a place where I am right. I must leave this place." Adam became afraid, for he had spoken in anger and he did not wish to be alone. Lilith felt strong and waved goodbye to Adam, calling to him, "I will find my own tree to climb."

Adam pleaded with God, "Do not leave me alone, but do not burden me with another Lilith. You promised me a perfect world. Create a woman who will be dependent on me, a woman who will recognize my importance."

And God created Eve.

Bonnie Feinman

Then the Lord said, "The outrage of Sodom and Gomorrah is so great, and their sin so grave! I will go down to see whether they have acted altogether according to the outcry that has reached Me...." (Genesis 18:20-22)

This midrash is based on a parable which is found in the Talmud, in Sanhedrin 109b:

A certain maiden gave some bread to a poor man (hiding it) in a pitcher. On the matter becoming known, they daubed her with honey and placed her on the parapet of the wall and the bees came and consumed her. Thus it is written, And the Lord said, Because the cry of Sodom and Gomorrah, etc.

Can any good be found in places such as Sodom and Gomorrah, where human beings treat one another so brutally?

> Beyond the city's horizon
> she waits, mute as a lake
> while straight ahead her daydream rumbles,
> warnings tumble from the sky;
> or is it those microscopic dwellers in her eye?

In Ribah's town they believed in arranged marriages. She would be bride of the bees. She was the golden bloom of Sodom, the fragrant cup of light in the stinking cave. To drink from her was any man's nocturnal wish. She walked through town, her flesh humming the black spirals of desire, but the only man she ever loved was a stranger. He had winged great distances to answer the call which she, unknown to herself, had given.

Now, the hospitality of Sodom and Gomorrah is well known. They even had a special bed just for guests. If a visitor was too short for the bed, they s-t-r-e-t-c-h-e-d his limbs like bread dough until he filled every corner. And if one was too tall, that was no problem either. They simply crushed him until he fit snugly as a sardine in a can on a shelf.

When the stranger arrived, Ribah didn't know who he was. She feared him as she had learned to fear all strangers.

"You must never trust an outsider," they hissed. "He is a savage wolf born in the wilds; you take him into your house, domesticate him with warmth and food, but who knows when the day will come, hunger gripping you both by the throat, that your precious dog will turn wolf on you before he himself starves?"

She had met him at the well. It was just as she had dreamed: she and her little sister, Deborah, vessels on their heads like crowns, would see a strange man by a tree. Almost a clown, almost an angel, his hair a ruddy cloud around his head, his eyes green as the river.

When the two sisters looked into the well, his eyes would stare back at them, moist and mysterious, asking for water. Ribah would hesitate to come near him. Deborah would go at once.

For the little one didn't understand the rule about strangers yet. She would go right up to him with her sparkling cup, eager to please, reaching out to touch his hair. Then she'd scamper back to Ribah in fright. Instinctively, she knew this man was taboo. She knew from his eyes, one gray delta and one green delta, outpourings from a river running deep in his brain.

Ribah saw him drinking her with his eyes, though it was the other's cup he held. Never had she been wanted so openly by any man. She ached to know him, to mount on his back and fly from home. Instead she turned away.

But these villagers could feel when anything alien entered their territory. The wind shifted slightly, the skin prickled up their backs, they couldn't laugh if they tried. A foreign presence made the inhabitants of Sodom and Gomorrah light one candle in the dark safety of their huts and chant with their families in a circle round the flame, as their grandparents had chanted before them and their grandparents before them:

> Ride not the back of the nightmare
> Honor not your succubi and incubi
> Believe not their tall tales of slumber
> Hear not their ravings of heat
> Focus on the gaze that pierces
> Turn it to rays of light
>
> All is changing, changing, changing
> All is changing, changing, changing
> See to the heart of every moment
> Fly on wings of being, being
> Fly on wings of being, being
> Fly on wings of Shekhinah

Not a soul remembered any longer what the strange words meant, but they chanted them anyway. To stop would anger the ancestors.

The mother of Ribah and Deborah gave them this warning in addition to the chant, for she knew that was not enough: "Strangers will come to you from afar, attracted by your exotic female smell. They will come like a herd of bees." Her voice broke but she continued, "You must turn your honey to venom before they sting you. A stranger's sting must not penetrate."

These words forced tears out of her eyes. Even as she stared straight at her daughters, her cheeks, neck, and throat soon were encased in saltwater glaze. Her garments were stiff. Ribah and Deborah watched their mother turn into a pillar of salt as the last tears crystallized in her eyes. She stood before them, a frozen memorial to sperm.

Her warning meant this: "The male body is the quintessence of strangeness. Sex signifies a brutal invasion of your native land by a foreign country." She couldn't stomach it, never having been wooed in the flesh, never even having had her own name. She was best known as Lot's wife. She tried to implant in her daughters a horror of rainbow sexuality, a loathing of purple pleasure and scarlet celebration. But the warning came too late.

For, when the stranger finally arrived, how could they resist his eyes which flowed from deepest rivers, his hair which was a Shekhinah cloud floating above his head, or his words which emanated from his heart and spoke to the heart of each daughter? When he asked for water, how could they refuse to give it to him?

So the villagers came to give Ribah her due, to marry her to the bees. They spirited her on their backs to the parapet of the wall of the city. Though it was the little sister who had given the stranger drink, Ribah was the one who had been initiated into the secrets of women. She should have known the taboo and yet she contaminated herself with a stranger.

"You have one last request," the villagers informed her.

"I wish only to speak with my sister before I am married," she said.

Deborah appeared from out of the midst of the hysterical crowd and Ribah spoke these last words to her:

"Deborah, we come from the same egg. Your dreams are my dreams, though we sleep in different skins. We reflect each other's mistaken identities—you call the stranger unto you with a lascivious finger while I repel him with a cold blast from my eyes.

"There is a man between us. He is our father and our brother and our husband. He is the bridge that binds us, do you see? And he is the gulf that separates us. Without him we are two vast chasms facing each other, dually concealing our buried root as if our line began with a wanton cat. But even when he is there, our feline eyes gleam in the dark, piercing through him till we stare straight into each other.

"Once you confided to me, sitting up in bed like Lilith in heat: I want lots and lots of babies, kneading your stomach with hands that love to bake. I saw you green, green as fields in spring and green as a pond swimming with water lilies. Fertility swarms in us both: in you a dripping hive, in me a buzzing that deafens.

"Deborah, give me your blessing for this marriage."

The one with the eager cup looked at her sister and nodded. Then she closed her eyes and murmured slowly these words:

My sister, may your cry be great in Sodom and Gomorrah
May it resound in the world beyond these walls
May you learn the secret of how to turn the sting to honey.

The villagers could wait no longer. They pushed Deborah

out of the way and anchored Ribah by the neck to a boulder, taunting, "Now try to lure the souls from men with your flesh songs." They smeared honey all over her body, laughing with their teeth, hungry wolves. And they left her.

"A plucked fruit, she'll soon rot." They laughed themselves back home, stumbling all the way, drunk from the deed and the thick smell of honey. Bees swarmed past them in droves.

Ribah lay on the gray wall. The sunset light was melting in the sky. She summoned up all the words of strength she could:

Before I lost my voice and my hands dangled clammy
    at my side
Before the cadaverous mists of dawn made the
    mountains sleeping beasts
Before the door opened and the ticking stopped
Before I looked inside my own face
Before I picked the fruit
Before I opened my mouth
Before I listened to the subtle stranger
Before I had a name
My marriage to the bees was already arranged:
I would cleave to the stranger no matter how painful
Though the villagers pluck on my fear like a lyre,
I'll turn their story of bees to a tale of love.

Then she heard the bees coming. MMMMMMMMMMM. It sounded like a Daleth—DDDDDDDDDDDDDDD and a Beth—BBBBBBBBBBBBBBB and a Resh—RRRRRRRR-RRRRRR.

Daleth is the Deleth, the Door. Beth is the Bayit, the House. Resh is Rosh, the Head.

The mouth is the door to the house of the head.

She opens her mouth and spawns the word, D'var: Daleth, Beth, Resh. The letters push out her mouth, forming a scarlet lily. The bees suck sweet nectar from this word and are transformed into a man. Her bridegroom is the stranger at the well.

They hold each other very close, breasts and arms and cheeks so close, her hair rushing down his back. They kiss and he plants seeds in her, numerous as stars. "I have been empty," trembles Ribah, "so empty." She shudders at the memory of a wind that used to scream through her without a face. "I want to fill you," he breathes; "I want you," he whispers.

Inside her, the iron door crumbles and fresh air carries tears on a slow river to his eyes.

Then Ribah sings to him: Your tongue glistens, not stinging with flesh frenzy but entering with the foreign word that leaps inside me. My frightened villagers warned of hot fat sliding off a strange tongue, burning and searing—on my gentle ear. I ache for your words dipped in salt sea water, soft and endless. You are no age, dripping as your first dawn, shimmering, blind, crawling back into my birth cave, back through the motherdark, deep into the blooddark sea of ultimate fish swarming like stars all singing all feeding all floating all fondling inside one glowing egg.

Penina V. Adelman

*Lot's wife looked back, and she turned into a pillar of salt.
(Genesis 19:26)*

Why did Lot's wife become a pillar of salt?

When the Angels of God came that morning to urge Lot, Tova, and their two daughters to hurry to leave Sodom before it was too late, Tova was already at work gathering their belongings.

She knew that her home and the homes of all of her friends were going to be destroyed. Tova pushed these thoughts from her mind. They were too painful. She must not think of what was coming. She must just get everything ready. "Let's see," she thought to herself, "we will need blankets, water jugs, oil, spices, flour. . . ." The list seemed endless. She sent her daughters to the kitchen to get the necessary food and utensils while she went from room to room collecting the things of value that could be carried.

As Tova picked up a bracelet, she remembered her friend, Naomi, who had given it to her. Dear Naomi who had always been there when Tova needed her. In a few hours, Naomi would be dead. Her children would be dead. Tears began to blur Tova's vision. She wiped her eyes on her sleeve as she hurried on into the next room. There, through the window, she saw her neighbor's children, Daniel and Sari, playing. They were really growing. She hadn't noticed how big they had gotten...soon they too would be dead. The tears came quickly now and spilled over onto her cheeks, but she didn't bother to dry them. They were too many.

Memories were forcing themselves into her mind. There was Rebekah who helped Tova just last week by taking care of Tova's family while she was sick. There was Shoshana, who always invited Tova and Lot over for holiday dinners, knowing that Tova's family lived far away. There were the neighbors across the street who came over to help whenever there was trouble. They were all going to die. Tova's head began to pound as the tears rolled down her face and onto the floor.

Tova couldn't understand why she and Lot were chosen to be saved. She knew they did their best to do what was right, but they weren't perfect. Who was? And what about the babies and innocent children? Why couldn't God just destroy the people who were really evil? Why destroy everyone?

Tova heard Lot and the men sent by God calling to her. She took a last look around, tightened her arms around her bundles, called to her daughters and ran out to meet them.

As they fled down the street, Tova heard one of the men say, "Flee for your life, do not look back." She felt something in her eye and as she brushed her hand across her face, she felt the salty residue that had been left by her tears. At that moment, Tova's heart was so heavy with sadness and pity for those who were left behind that she could go no further. She turned to look back for one last time.

God saw Tova and felt her anguish and compassion. God knew that Tova could never be happy knowing she had survived while everyone else had been killed. God knew then what to do. As Tova turned to look back, God changed her into a pillar of salt. For just as Tova's tears evaporated leaving their salty residue, Tova's spirit evaporated, leaving forever a monument to her deep feelings of love and caring—a monument made from the condensation of Tova's compassion.

Arlene Saidman

Lot's wife looked back, and she turned into a pillar of salt. (Genesis 19:26)

Why is Lot's wife behind her husband? Why does she turn to salt?

It has become unbearable here. Wild strangers beat down our door at night and try to rape everything in sight: man, woman, and beast. I have begged Lot to leave, to move to the country, to the hills, anywhere, away from this horrible place. It must be better elsewhere. But he doesn't listen. He makes the decisions in this family. I sometimes think it is because I would have us go that he, stubbornly, decides to stay. I fear for my tender daughters and their new husbands. What kind of place is this to raise their children? Perhaps if I keep quiet Lot will realize that the best course is for us to flee. Perhaps he'll forget that it was my idea. Let my desires and dreams be expunged entirely from the record—I don't care—anything to get out of this city.

All at once Lot has changed his mind. My ploy must have worked. Now I can't move fast enough for him. My fingers are too slow in packing. Where has all this urgency come from? I run behind him, and finally, catching up, walk behind him, as is our custom here. We plod through the dusty desert, leaving the noise of the city in back of us. Lot kicks up fans of dust that settle in my hair. A wheel of dried myrtle branches tumbles along in front of us. There is a rumor that the whole metropolis behind us is going to be set aflame. (I had a dream like this, once: little girls, agents of God, set fire to the brothels and idol shrines. Sodom and Gomorrah turned to ashes.) We don't utter a word to each other. I can hear my footfalls in the sand; with each step excitement builds. Onward to the future, to a better life, to a place where men don't behave as animals.

My feet carry me forward, into my dreams of the future. Perhaps we will arrive at a magical place where wives do not walk behind, where our ideas are acknowledged, where the births of girls are celebrated, where judges listen to the testimony of women, where barren wives are not forsaken ... perhaps I will be able to remember my name there. (I know it must be something other than Lot's Wife, but what?) The sun settles on the top of my head and burns. I wipe perspiration from my temples. As we press onward, the past takes on an air of unreality. Can such a miserable place really have existed?

I want to steal a look backward, just to assure myself that the rumors are true. I turn and, yes! Wisps of smoke are beginning to rise! I pause on the brink of reeling around again, to search the landscape of desert in front of Lot, to try to find signs of a better life. But I hesitate. I cannot make myself turn around again. Suppose our destination merely resembles our point of origin?

In this moment of hesitation, I feel myself transformed. I can move neither backward nor forward, nor do I wish to move any longer. The destination that I seek does not yet exist. Until the time has come to advance, I feel I must remain in this place that is all my own, in this patch of desert that I now mark as an obelisk.

Wives scoop me up to preserve their meats and spice their soups. I float suspended in the lake and make children buoyant so that they do not drown. I am replenished by the tears shed by mothers grieving for their sons killed in battle. And I wait, I wait, to become a person at last.

Susan Gross

A midrash on Genesis chapter 21, verses 1-14.

What caused Abraham's uncharacteristically cruel and irresponsible behavior toward his son and concubine? And were Abraham and Sarah really a patriarchal couple?

Ninety-year-old Sarah has given birth to a son. They call him Yitzchak because it's an event to laugh about. But Sarah isn't quite sure if people will laugh with her, helping her rejoice in her unexpected motherhood, or if they will laugh at her, making fun of her and of her old husband.

Nor is she sure about Hagar's son, Ishmael. Is he laughing at her or at her beloved child, Yitzchak? But she is too tense and sensitive to linger over these questions. She wants that handmaiden and her son out of her house, and she makes that very clear to Abraham, fully expecting to be heard by him.

Most surprising is Abraham's reaction. This man of action becomes depressed over Sarah's demand. This is the first and only time in the long and detailed saga of Abraham's life that we see him unable to make a forthright decision and act on it immediately. In war, protection of kinsmen, domestic quarrels, issues of justice—even challenging God —Abraham never sat around stewing, nor did he wait for God to bail him out. He always took the initiative, doing what was right or necessary.

But here it seems that Abraham has been making invalid claims. He has been acting as if God made a covenant with him alone—when in fact, God had a covenant with both Abraham and Sarah. It is their child—and not any child of Abraham's—that is to carry on the covenant, as God tells him in a previous chapter (Gen. 17:19,21). Confused and in conflict about his authority, he must have given Ishmael and Hagar the feeling that it was all up to him, and that they had reason to expect the tide to turn in their favor.

But Sarah is not the submissive little wife of a patriarch. She is a powerful woman, well aware of her equality in the covenant (as are all the pre-Mosaic women in the Bible, down to and including Moses' sister Miriam). So, Sarah asserts her equal position, and Abraham becomes dejected and paralyzed. God has to step in and tell him what to do, which is simply: "Do what Sarah tells you."

Abraham obeys, but not in his usual forthright and whole-hearted way. In the process, he fails as he has never failed before. He sends his concubine and his son out into the desert without sufficiently providing for them. Of course, God takes over, because God has made a promise to Hagar, too. But that does not exonerate Abraham from the guilt of having exposed Hagar and Ishmael to starvation and death.

What accounts for Abraham's failure? When read without the blinders of later patriarchal interpretations, the answer seems clear: Abraham fails as a father because he does not want to share the duties and privileges of parenthood with his wife, Sarah. Thinking of himself as the only one with whom God made the covenant, he forgets that God and Sarah were also covenanted. This presumptuousness involves him in shaky claims, and he loses authority in his household. It is thus his patriarchal pride that brings about his personal failure, which, but for God's intervention, would have engendered a family tragedy.

For us, the descendants of Abraham and Sarah, an unbiased reading of these biblical passages will reveal the non-patriarchal meaning of the story, affirming the equal status for men and women in the covenant with God, a meaning beclouded by later interpretations of the tradition.

Esther K. Ticktin

And He said, "Take your son, your favored one, Isaac, whom you love, and go to the land of Moriah, and offer him there as a burnt offering...." (Genesis 22:2)

Where was Sarah?

The Angel of God came to Sarah and said, "Take your son, Isaac, up to the mountain and build an altar and give him as an offering to prove that you are loyal and fear God."

Sarah covered her eyes because she was afraid to look upon the face of God's Angel, and she shook her head. "No. I cannot sacrifice my son. He is God's gift to me. He is too precious."

All night Sarah could not sleep. Her first thought was to run away with Isaac to the desert and hide. But in her heart she knew that God sees and knows all. She then thought she would find another child among the desert people to exchange for Isaac, but she knew that the deception would be discovered. When she arose from her bed the following morning, she learned that Abraham and Isaac and two of their followers had left the camp, and she understood that the Angel had also appeared to Abraham and that he had left with Isaac to do God's bidding.

She cried out to the Lord, "Oh, Master of the World, Creator of the Universe, hear my prayer. Have You forgotten that You gave me a child only after I had waited ninety years? Have You forgotten that You Yourself told me that I would bear an heir to our people, that through Your doing Abraham's son would become head of Your nation? Have You forgotten that special mother's love for her child? Dear God, spare my son. Do not permit Abraham to slay him. Take me for Your peace offering. I go willingly —please stay the hand of Abraham."

As she cried these words, God heard them and caused a ram to appear in the thicket, and the Angel spoke to Abraham. "Untie Isaac and take this ram for the burnt offering, for God has heard the heart of Mother Sarah."

Sylvia Karzen

A midrash on Genesis chapter 22.

What was Sarah doing while Abraham prepared to sacrifice their son Isaac?

Sarah lay quietly in the tent. It was late and Abraham had fallen asleep long before. She tried to picture the stars as she listened to the gentle breeze against the tent flaps. Just now she was not thinking about the occasional difficulties of life in the wilderness. Instead, its soft beauty enfolded and comforted her.

She sat up slowly, so as not to wake Abraham. Stretching a bit, she looked down at her years-worn body and smiled. For every wrinkle there was a story, and, as she silently chuckled, after 127 years she certainly had her share of "stories." She thought of her son Isaac, who lay in a tent nearby. He was, perhaps, her favorite "story," having come when she felt her womb too old for such a blessing. She recalled the three men who had come to announce Isaac's birth, and how she had laughed at them until Elohim had reassured her. Truly Elohim could have given her no greater happiness than she had gleaned from Isaac these past years. She whispered a prayer of thanks, rolled over on her mat, and contentedly went back to sleep.

She had not dozed long when she was awakened by Abraham stirring in his sleep. With a sudden jerk he sat up and called, *"Hineni."** Sarah knew that such a word was addressed to Elohim alone. She was not surprised when Abraham rose to stand beneath the stars near the camp's altar. She could see the outline of his shadow on the side of the tent and leaned toward it trying to share in this latest revelation.

At first what she heard made little sense. Abraham's usually strong, even voice was laced with anger, then reluctance, then acceptance. Though she could only hear Abraham's responses, she began to understand that Elohim had requested something involving Isaac.

She listened more intently. For a moment she thought she heard the word sacrifice, but she knew she must be mistaken. Then she heard it again, this time coming as a choking sob from deep within Abraham's throat. Her whole body tingled with horror. This was impossible—a nightmare. Elohim could not have requested that Abraham sacrifice her only son. Her mind rebelled with a torrent of defenses. Elohim had given her Isaac. Certainly it was far from Divine to take this special gift from her now, and without even addressing her directly! She must have misunderstood.

Abraham returned to the tent. Sarah had never seen him gripped with such sadness, not even when they were commanded to leave the land where they were born or on that awful day Sodom was destroyed. She knew she had not been mistaken. She longed to hold Abraham in her arms, to cry

---

* *"Here I am."*

together, to beg him not to obey, but his eyes were distant and she was afraid. She had been excluded from hearing the voice and knew she was powerless to interfere in what passed between Elohim and Abraham. She felt guilty for having tried to eavesdrop, and for a moment she thought this strange command was her punishment. Yet, she had not been so evil as to deserve the loss of her only son. Surely Elohim had not abandoned all justice.

She lay in the dark, tense and empty and disbelieving. She could not even cry. It was as if, with losing Isaac, she was emptied of all emotion. This could not be real. An urgent need to see Isaac burned within her. Perhaps it was a need to say goodbye. If she left the tent, Abraham would question her, for though he lay still he certainly could not be asleep. She was hardly in the mood to discuss the matter with him, but could not bear to lie beside him any longer. She thought angrily, "I do not care what he thinks. He is the one willing to sacrifice Isaac. He is the guilty one."

She rose quickly, eager to escape the confinement of the tent. Confused, she did not go directly to Isaac's tent, but instead wandered the camp. She passed the sheep and goats, calmly resting, well cared for, just as Elohim commanded. She looked at the mountains in the distance, dimly shadowed in moonlight. Their awesomeness penetrated her through, to fill the emptiness inside. She would not believe that the Elohim of these mountains, Elohim who protected them in the journeys, Elohim who had given her Isaac, would now take him away. Over and over she asked herself how it could be, convinced that if she asked enough times, an answer would come. She rested on a rock, knowing the dawn of the day on which her son would be sacrificed continued its relentless approach. "Sacrifice for what?" she thought. She sat until she could sit no longer and again wandered the camp aimlessly.

She shuddered as she approached the altar where Abraham had agreed to obey Elohim's unthinkable command. Abraham's special knife leaned against one side. Her insides contracted with disgust as she thought of it against Isaac's throat. She pictured all the sacrifices she had witnessed. They seemed ugly now. Yet, something from those pictures pressed inside her. The sacrifices had not always seemed ugly. They had been strong symbols of commitment—a sign of appreciation for Elohim's protection and guidance. Could Elohim be looking for that kind of sign now? Had they given Elohim reason to doubt their commitment? What event could be so great that Elohim would seek reassurance from them, and why now, and why involve Isaac? Slowly her stream of questions evolved into a clear vision.

Recollections of the times Elohim had touched their lives permeated her thoughts—the joyous memories brought an unintended smile to her lips. She remembered the promises Elohim had made to them, promises that their offspring would inherit this land and become a great nation. It had been many years since she had thought about that promise. She had always assumed that Isaac would follow in his father's footsteps as head of the tribe, but she had never considered just how Isaac would inherit his parents' commitment to serving Elohim. She had known since Isaac's birth that she and Abraham were not destined to live much longer. If they were to pass on the Covenant to their son, it would have to be soon. Elohim's strange command was the sign that the time had arrived. From their simple world would grow a great people, proudly bound to Elohim just as they had been.

Her heart pounded at the thought of such responsibility. The future of the ideals they had learned from Elohim depended on their actions now. She was no longer surprised that Elohim wished reaffirmation of their commitment.

Everything made sense now. What greater test for Abraham than to give up his son, or for Isaac to give up his life. She understood that Elohim did not really intend for Isaac to die. She also understood that she was Elohim's tool to prevent Isaac's death. She returned to the tent just before the first light of dawn crept from behind the mountains. She entered quietly and pretended to sleep, hoping Abraham would not question her absence, for she would be tempted to share her vision and to do so would ruin his chance to prove himself.

In the morning Abraham announced that he was going to Moriah with Isaac. He did not explain why. He gathered a few men, adequate supplies for the three-day journey, and departed without saying goodbye. Sarah understood his silence. As soon as he was out of sight she prepared for her own journey. She, too, took supplies enough for the trip and also the finest ram in camp.

For the first days she followed Abraham's tracks, but upon approaching Moriah she was careful to stay opposite the side of the mountain where Abraham had set up camp. The sun had risen just a short time earlier, and the morning breeze cooled her as she walked up the mountain, ram in tow. When she could no longer catch her breath, she released the ram and shooed it up the slope. As she watched it run up to the heights where she knew Abraham and Isaac would be, she smiled. With the contentment that comes from completing an arduous task, Sarah lay down in the grass and drifted into a peaceful sleep.

When she awoke, the sun was already low in the sky. Looking out over the hills, she could see Abraham and Isaac heading home. She was proud of Isaac, knowing he would carry on the Covenant with Elohim his parents had established. She returned to the foot of the hill and sent her party after them. She remained behind, still tired from the journey.

And the life of Sarah was a hundred and seven
and twenty years; these were the years of the life
of Sarah. (Genesis 23:1)

Faith Rogow

Author's Note: I wrote this several years before I had the
privilege of reading Savina Teubal's *Sarah The Priestess*.
Were I to approach the text now, I would write a completely
different story. Still, I believe this version contains perspectives which challenge the norm and challenge the reader to
think from a woman's perspective, so I am not willing to
abandon it altogether.

They called Rebekah and said to her, "Will you go with this man?" And she said, "I will." (Genesis 24:58)

What enabled Rebekah to decide to leave her family and to adjust to a new life with Isaac and his clan, all strangers to her?

Beneath Rebekah's pleasant demeanor, there was a layer of sadness that thickened with time. No one suspected it, least of all Isaac. He was aware of a certain distance between them, but he simply accepted this as part of the character of a beautiful woman—a woman more beautiful than he had ever dared to imagine as his wife—and Isaac never probed any further.

When Abraham's messenger first encountered Rebekah at the well, there had been so much excitement. It was always an event when someone came from another region. Then, when the messenger had sought her out and the object of his journey had become clear—to find a wife for Abraham's heir—she had been flattered indeed and filled with a sense of importance and destiny that had shut out any other feelings. Even her family had put no obstacle in her way, leaving the decision completely to her. Rebekah had been full of excitement and a sense of adventure. She had had no question then.

If only they had tried to stop her! How she missed her family and all her own people. Especially her friends. How wonderful it had been each day to draw water from the well and meet all of them there. Her friend Brine had always had a secret to tell her. Rebekah had had a crush on Brine's older brother, Benjamin. Brine had always had something special to report about what he had said or done that Rebekah could hardly wait to hear. Or they would gossip about their other friends and watch the younger children at play amidst the cackling hens with the camels in the background. It had been a lively scene indeed!

How she wished she could be back there now. Here, in her new surroundings, there was a well, too. But it was not the same. Rebekah was supposed to let a servant draw the water even if she came along. And when she did go to the well, the other women showed respect for her status as Abraham's daughter-in-law. There was a distance between them. How little she had realized that her new position would have such consequences.

One day, as Rebekah brooded alone in the privacy of her tent, she heard a voice speak to her. It seemed to come from behind, but when she turned around, she saw no one. Again the voice addressed her: Rebekah, do not grieve. You must be patient. For you not only will give birth to strong men, but you will be the one to choose Isaac's heir, and the next leader of the tribes of Israel.

And then, the voice was gone. Rebekah knew that God has spoken to her and that God had chosen her for a special destiny.

Helen Gotkowitz

12

Rebekah then took the best clothes of her older son Esau, which were there in the house, and had her younger son Jacob put them on; and she covered his hands and the hairless part of his neck with the skins of the kids. Then she put in the hands of her son Jacob the dish and the bread that she had prepared. (Genesis 27:15-17)

What induced Rebekah to deceive her husband and betray her elder son?

Say you have twins
and one's a bear of a boy
who roars in all sweaty from hunting
and hugs you half to death
and grabs his supper, and chases off
after the girls

and his father's crazy about him.

And the other's the quiet kind
who hangs around the house
and takes care of his mama

and the wrong one's born first.

It was an inspiration: I just said,
Seize the day, Jacob;
your brother's nowhere around,
go put on his good sheepskins,
get yourself blessed,
and for God's sake, don't tell Papa.

Isaac was furious
and Esau took it harder than I expected.

Well, what was I to do? Trust my old age
to that wild man and his Hittites?
Who knows—maybe if I had pushed harder
Jacob might have come out first.

Anyway, as I always say,
what difference will it make in a hundred years?

Barbara D. Holender

And Rachel said, "A fateful contest I waged with my sister, and I have prevailed." So she named him Naphtali. (Genesis 30:8)

What was the struggle with her sister, Leah, that Rachel was referring to, and why did she want to name her child in reference to that experience?

To be sisters married to the same man was no easy thing. It was one thing to learn to share the love of parents; to share a husband was another matter altogether. For years, Rachel and Leah had been locked in struggle to win Jacob's love and to produce the sons who would one day be the fathers of the tribes of Israel. Where once they had been close confidantes, even allies, now Leah and Rachel vied to outdo the other and each felt the other prevailed.

Leah knew Jacob's first love was for Rachel alone. "Maybe with time..." she thought, "maybe if I bear him sons...he will one day see me for what I am and love me." And so she continued to hope, son after son after son. But still she felt hollow inside.

Rachel loved Jacob and knew he returned that love. But as the years passed and she remained childless, the love she and Jacob shared left her less and less fulfilled. "Give me children or else I die," she cried to Jacob. Jacob answered her with anger: "Am I in God's stead withholding from you fruit of the womb?"

Rachel finally gave Jacob her handmaid, Bilhah, in the hopes that at least through her she might bear sons. When Bilhah bore a son to Jacob, Rachel named him Dan saying "God has judged me; God has heeded my plea and given me a son." But she had not believed her own words then and did not know that Bilhah was about to bear Jacob a second child. "If it is a son, what should I name him?" Rachel wondered. While others in her place might have rejoiced, her heart was heavy. These were not *her* children as they would be to a birth mother.

As bitter as she felt toward Leah, though, Rachel knew her childlessness was not Leah's fault. And she knew Jacob was right; he was not in God's stead. So she turned to God. For years Rachel had prayed to God to fill her womb. Now her prayers took on the tone of a challenge. "What is it You want from me, God? Why should my sister be blessed with children, and my handmaid too, and still after so many years I stand childless? Is there some deficiency in me? Isn't it enough I've had to share the husband I've loved since my youth with my older sister? And yet with each passing year Leah has more to show for his love than I! God how I hate her!" And with the last words, Rachel began to weep.

It had not always been this way. Rachel remembered the long mornings she and Leah had spent working together in the kitchen of their father's home, their long walks to and from the well, singing the songs their mother had taught them, talking away the hours. How often they had wondered how much they would be able to see each other once they were each married and occupied with their own families and household. "Little did we know," Rachel laughed bitterly. "Little did we know."

Jacob had it easy, she thought to herself. When he had problems with his brother he just did what he had to do. He left his brother behind and went on with his life. What kind of an option was that for her? If she were to leave, she would also lose Jacob. Besides, with all her sons, Leah was secure in Jacob's household.

No, she did not have the choice Jacob had had. But then again, she knew how he was still plagued with thoughts of his brother. Who was Esau now, twenty years after Jacob had outsmarted him and grabbed their father's blessing for the firstborn? Did Esau still want to destroy him? Had Jacob done the right thing allowing himself to be coaxed by his mother to trick his brother and father? His mother had been so sure, so strong and reassuring. Would Esau ever forgive him? Rachel knew that Jacob still suffered sleepless nights, so tortured were his thoughts. Someday, Rachel felt deep within her heart, Jacob would again have to confront Esau. What would happen then God only knew. Meanwhile, Rachel realized Jacob was still locked in struggle with his brother, in a stranglehold embrace he had not managed to escape when he had fled his parents' home so many years before.

Rachel sighed. No, it would never be easy, but for her it was clear that she and her sister were in this together. It wasn't either/or. Neither she nor Leah would just walk out of this situation. But why couldn't she bear a child? Why should Leah be the one to have it all, she thought bitterly? And then she stopped short.

In her own pain she had grown so estranged from Leah, she had become the one with weak eyes. She realized with a start that Leah, too, must still be in pain. She remembered

Leah's shame at having been pushed by their father to share Jacob's wedding bed disguised as Rachel, how Leah had hardly been able to face her. She remembered suddenly the first three of Leah's births and namings: "Reuven, for surely the Lord has looked upon my affliction and now therefore my husband will love me." Then "Shimon, because the Lord has heard that I was hated, he has therefore given me this son also." And then "Levi, now this time my husband will be joined to me because I have borne him three sons."

No, Leah was not happy either. Each of them seemed to have what the other wanted. Each was left with a yearning. "We may not be able to rid ourselves of these longings," Rachel thought. "But perhaps we can find a way to be sisters again."

Only then did Rachel recall her mother's words from so many years before. God's prophecy to Rebekah before Esau's and Jacob's birth had been passed on to Rachel and Leah: "Two nations are in your womb; two people shall be separated from your bowels, and the one people shall be stronger than the other, and the elder shall serve the younger." "The one shall be stronger than the other," the mother had said. "So they will think. But the secret truth contained within is that in the bonding that grows from reconciliation will there be true strength."

Rachel had assumed her mother's words applied only to Jacob and Esau and their descendants. Now she knew what she would name Bilhah's baby if it were to be another boy: "Naphtali," she thought, "for with wrestlings of God have I wrestled with my sister and I have persevered."

Rachel arose and with painful and pleasant memories, with new questions and with hope, she headed for Leah's tent.

Rabbi Ruth H. Sohn

Now Dinah, the daughter whom Leah had borne to Jacob, went out to meet the women of the land. (Genesis 34:1)

Who were these women and why did Dina go to meet them?

Dina, daughter of Leah, whose father was Yaakov, heard from her servant about the monthly meetings of the desert women. Dina longed to go, because B'elilah spoke intensely of the powers that were revealed during the gatherings. However, Dina was still a young girl and her bride price had not been negotiated. She begged B'elilah time and time again to take her just once. B'elilah knew it wasn't allowed, yet she recognized Dina's creative urge and knew she must be taught soon.

Finally, late one moonless night, Dina and B'elilah slipped out of the camp. *Dina went out to meet the women of the land.* They traveled silently, listening to the sound of desert animals along the way. The sky, brilliantly spangled with stars, provided the necessary light for the journey.

B'elilah explained along the way that men were not allowed in the camp of the women, for the initiation rites of the women must be protected. After all, it was through the teachings of the female cycle that all life was sustained. Young women had to learn the rhythms of their bodies as they tuned to the lunar light. A woman must know when her scents were ripe to seduce men and when her time of fertility had arrived. Oils were perfumed with the flowers of the desert, herbs were brewed to lengthen the time for conception, and potions were prepared to induce the dreams of sacred vision. These secrets had been relayed from mother to daughter for many years and must be maintained.

Dina and B'elilah arrived at the camp at the first signs of dawn. From the top of the ridge, Dina gasped at the huge ring of tents nestled among the dunes. As they descended the side of the great valley, many voices greeted them. "Welcome, sisters of the Mother!" "Our friend B'elilah brings a young woman." "Come feast and prepare with us!" "Welcome!"

Dina and B'elilah were escorted to a tent where they cleansed themselves from the journey and anointed their bodies with perfumes of wild sage. Dressed in ceremonial robes brought by B'elilah, they joined the other women seated in a large circle. Some were chanting, some offering silent prayers, some wailing the names of G-d into the starry night. Some had been meditating for three days in preparation for the gathering. Slowly, the dawn broke and the soft murmurings grew louder. The chanting intensified and the drums began to pound insistently.

As Dina watched in amazement, some of the women slowly rose to their feet and began to dance to the drums. The rhythm became faster as more bodies rose to weave in and out to the music. Dina, watching them move, began to feel the vibrations of the beat through her body, too. As if an uncontrollable force possessed her, she rose to lose herself in the maze of dancing, sweating, ecstatic energy.

After what seemed like hours, she felt a strange sweating. Looking down, she noticed her darkly stained gown. "I have finally begun my bleeding," Dina noted to herself. "So this is the power of the ritual."

Suddenly, a cry was heard from one of the corner guards. "Men in the camp!" Camels and riders raced into the circle of the women. The men had been watching from the top of the dunes! They had seen the sacred circle!

Dina was confused. She stood rooted in fear as a camel charged in her direction. Pulling up directly in front of her, the young rider in regal robes locked eyes with Dina. She returned his gaze boldly, noticing his striking features. Suddenly, he grabbed her arm, and swinging her up behind him, rode off with her! When this happened, the other men fled quickly.

The women were shocked, bruised, and bewildered. It was not the first time men had raided the camp, but it was the first time they had captured someone so young! B'elilah was beside herself in fear of her own worthless life. A plan was needed to get Dina back!

The women called for volunteers to set out after her. They gathered water, stones, pots, and pans for the journey. The men had been recognized as Hivites, whose king was Hamor. Shechem, his son, had captured Dina. The women would bring her back.

When they arrived at the tent of Shechem, prince of the land, thirsty, tired, and angry, the women surrounded his tent and began to beat their pots and pans with stones. They screamed and cursed and called the coward to come out. They sang and chanted and began to challenge and taunt his guards. "Your prince is a weak man that he must steal women. Come out, Shechem, or not one woman will lie peacefully with a man in your city again!" They rattled their utensils and spat on the ground.

The flap of the tent opened and Dina emerged. Her dress was torn, and her hair was matted, but she appeared unhurt. "Why do you assume I was stolen against my will? I chose this man as surely as he chose me. Now that I am a woman I may do as I like."

B'elilah was scornful. "That's what you think! Wait till your brothers hear about this. You are still my responsibility. I took you away from your family, and now I cannot face them without fear for my life. How can I tell your brothers you willingly went with a Canaanite? Listen to me now, Dina! If you don't return with me, I will go back there and say he took you by force. How else can I explain your sudden absence? Not to mention the loss of your virginity? I am sorry. I see you have made your choice, but I cannot face my masters without telling them thus."

And Dina said, "Do what you must do."

And so it was that the story came down to us that Dina went out to meet the women of the land, and was raped at the hands of Shechem, who loved her.

Rayzel Robinson
Margot Azen

A midrash on Genesis chapter 34.

How did Dina feel about the events that transpired? What, in other words, would Genesis 34 look like if it were told from Dina's point of view?

The sun had already set, yet Dina still heard their cries—the women, crying from pain and humiliation; the children, dazed, afraid to move, afraid that if they did, they'd be raped like their mothers, or killed like their fathers. Dina covered her ears and closed her eyes, wishing that she'd only imagined the screams of the Canaanites. How could she have lived with her brothers for all of those years, yet not really known them? How could they have acted so wantonly, so cruelly? When Jacob, their father, angrily asked them why they had done what they had done, they answered that it was because Shechem had raped Dina, treating her as a harlot. They had acted, they said, to defend her honor. But none of them had asked her how *she* felt. She suspected that none of them cared.

She hadn't asked to be raped. It was painful, but mercifully, brief. When it was over, she opened her eyes and saw

Shechem looking at her, tears trickling down his cheeks, ashamed and bewildered by his actions. He told her he loved her; she needed to believe him. When her father and brothers agreed that she could marry him, she wept with relief. She didn't love Shechem; the memory of his assault was still too fresh, yet he had said that he loved her and, perhaps now that she was no longer a virgin, might well be the only man who would ever love her, the only man who would ever want to make her his bride. For three days, she lived in his home. The Canaanite women whom she knew, having heard of her betrothal, came to see her. She met Shechem's father and his mother, his brothers and sisters, and began to feel that in time she could be happy. She knew that she could still visit her family, and Shechem assured her that she could still worship her God.

And then, early that morning, she awoke to the sound of Shechem's cries. She ran to find him lying next to his father in a pool of blood. She looked up and saw her brothers, Simeon and Levi, their swords dripping with blood, their faces gleaming with triumph. They brutally grabbed her and took her home, barely looking at her, hardly speaking. Perhaps they killed the Hivites to make their conquest of Canaan easier. They didn't know the Canaanites as she did. Nor did they want to. They only knew that God has promised the land to them, and that it would be theirs, one way or another. How convenient to talk of murder as revenge, as redeeming their sister's honor. To revenge her honor? She hardly thought so. Relegated to silence, still haunted by the cries of the Canaanites, Dina wrapped her arms around her chest, slowly rocking back and forth, shedding tears of shame and sorrow.

Ellen M. Umansky

16

The daughter of Pharaoh came down to bathe in the Nile, while her maidens walked along the riverside. She saw the basket among the reeds and sent her slave girl to fetch it. (Exodus 2:5)

How did Pharaoh's daughter end up casting her fate with the Hebrew people?

Miriam had always been a visionary girl, Thermutis thought, as her attendants prepared the bathing materials. If only her vision would not fail them this morning. Distractedly, she played with her Isis-ankh pendant and held her breath. Would their plan really work...and had she made the right decision?

It seemed only yesterday that Thermutis had learned that the Pharaoh had decided to kill all male Hebrew babies. Even though she had become accustomed to her father's fits of madness, she was shocked. His magicians had told him the Hebrew slaves were to be freed by a man-child as yet unborn, but everyone knew they'd say anything to stay in favor. She couldn't take any more; at the age of 16, she had to find a way out of this life that was suffocating her as surely as if she herself were a slave.

* * *

Since the time she was old enough to walk, Miriam had come daily to the palace with her mother, Yocheved, the Hebrew midwife. This past winter she had become a favorite serving-maid of the Lady Thermutis, and had begun to live at the palace in the servant-quarters. One day, however, after a visit home, Miriam seemed especially worried. That evening, Thermutis kept her behind as the other attendants left, and asked why she seemed so upset. Miriam, after much hesitation, revealed that Yocheved was pregnant. She told Thermutis about her dreams: that it was a boy-baby, that he shone with light. . . vivid strange dreams about mountains and water, about drowning, and one with a huge crowd of people around him, expectant and full of wonder. "I have to save him! I'm the only one, and this is my only chance!" she cried out. Suddenly, realizing to whom she was talking, she drew back. Without thinking, Thermutis reached out and held her close, knowing that Miriam was right, and that somehow this was *her* chance as well.

The two women whispered late into the night, listening for spies and exploring possible plans. There was no chance that a male child would remain undiscovered, for there were informers in each Hebrew camp who kept an eye on every pregnant woman, waiting for the birth. The searches and seizures were constant, with the sounds of mothers and sisters shrieking as children were taken from their arms. Somehow they had to find a way, soon, to spirit the baby out of the slave-camp before anyone knew he was alive. Yocheved was already five months pregnant.

In the weeks of worry that followed, Thermutis found herself developing a sympathy with Miriam and her people that she hadn't imagined possible. Hearing the stories that Miriam shared with her nightly, she began to feel as if she were almost a part of Miriam's family and friends, these Hebrews, who with their separate language and stubborn pride, seemed as if they had become slaves only last week instead of hundreds of years before. Slowly, Thermutis grew to appreciate the history of this people that she had been told had no history.

One night, as the friends came up with plan after unworkable plan, Thermutis suddenly knew what to do. Somehow, *she* would take the baby, raise him as her own, and give him back to his people when he was grown. It felt right, but seemed impossible—how would they convince Yocheved to let him grow up amidst the decadence of palace life? How would they get him into the palace in the first place? And what would happen when people realized that the daughter of the Pharaoh had adopted a Hebrew slave-baby? At least she still had one of the ancient privileges of the royal women: that of selecting her own mate, and her own child if she so chose. Miriam was not overly impressed by the plan, but she did agree to speak to Yocheved. All that remained was to figure out how to get the baby into the palace.

When Miriam returned from her next visit home, she told Thermutis that the baby had been born early—almost three months early, and it *was* a boy. Even more strange: after the birth, the room itself had been filled with light, just as in Miriam's dream. Fortunately, Yocheved had stayed silent throughout the birth, and there was a chance they would outwit the informers for a few months. But then what?

Three new-moons later, the knock on the door came. By good fortune, Miriam was at home, and she quickly grabbed the child and escaped through the back room. She placed him in a basket that Yocheved had prepared, and hid him in the reeds of the river, away from the slave-camp.

It was time for the two friends to put their plan into action. While Miriam spent more and more time away from the palace, visiting the child in the reeds and helping Yocheved at home, Thermutis threw herself into the planning for the spring Sed festival, three weeks hence. As eldest daughter of the Pharaoh, she was expected to play the Goddess Isis, and she hoped that if she appeared involved and excited, the Pharaoh might be favorably disposed when it came time for her to adopt the child.

* * *

When the day came, the plan was for Thermutis to go down to the river with her serving-ladies as usual to bathe and dress for the festivities. At some point, she would "notice" the basket, and ask one of her slave girls to bring it to her. She would open it, "fall in love" with the baby, and in a fit of imperiously spoiled behavior, insist on bringing it home with her.

Leaving the palace, she attempted to appear calm, even bored, but her breath caught with excitement. Her maidens were spread out behind her, gossiping and carrying baskets of ointments, cosmetics and perfumes, fruit and cakes, and the Goddess-gown and moon-shaped headdress that she would wear for the festival. As she descended the wide steps that led directly from the palace down to the Nile, she looked out over the water, and saw the early morning sun shining across it like gold. Thermutis breathed carefully; all was going well so far. She approached the water, and her maidservants helped her to undress; she hoped they would think her shivering was due to the coolness of the air. But as Thermutis stepped into the river, the water was slightly warm, and it felt as if she were re-entering the womb of the Mother. Standing breast deep in the water, she could no longer hear the voices of her attendants or the calling of the river birds. It seemed to her that the water had become a river of light, awaiting this moment, calling her to immerse her whole being in it. She sank down, lifting her feet from the sandy bottom, letting the light and the water enter her through every pore, through her mouth, her eyes, her ears, her womb. Her hair floated out around her, and from the center of her own silence she heard a voice calling her by a new name. "Bityah! Bityah!"—the voice echoed through her, and she felt enveloped in breath, bathed in sound and light, daughter of One infinitely larger and more within her than any god or goddess she had yet known.

* * *

After an eternity, she rose again out of the water, cleansed and alive. Looking at the river with new eyes, she saw the basket nearby, as they had planned. It was brought to her, and when she opened it, everyone could see the child inside, crying. But she alone saw the light surrounding the baby, like the light of the river, and she knew that she and Miriam had indeed chosen the right path. . . .

Traditional midrash, based on First Chronicles 4:19, states that Bityah ("daughter of God") was the name taken by Pharaoh's daughter, Thermutis, when she left Egypt as part of the Hebrew Exodus.

Roxane Neal

And Moses went down to the people and spoke to them. God spoke all these words, saying....'' (Exodus 19:25 - 20:1)

How did the women react to the giving of the Torah?

When Moses returned with the Torah and began interpreting its meaning to the leaders of the community, the women objected. They separated themselves to the side of the camp and began to talk, one to another. Said one, ''One of us is made responsible for Adam's sin. The loss of paradise sounds as though it is entirely our fault. This will not look good for us.''

Another said, ''We know so many wonderful women. Why are we scarcely mentioned? Where are our teachers, our prophets, our warriors, our heroes? If there are not more of these described, how will our daughters learn how to become like them?''

One woman, on her way toward becoming an accomplished writer, was searching through the text to see whether one of her own kind had contributed to it. She shook her head in disappointment. ''Of all our poets, why is there only one here mentioned?'' Another woman, soon to give birth, pushed forward. ''And our mothers. One is a manipulator who tricks her husband. And another of these mothers sounds so pathetic—always weeping. All in all, except for Deborah, not one of the women in this book appears to be really strong or impressive.''

Then came forward a young, eager woman newly widowed. ''Why are you worrying about the characters in these stories? What about its politics, its laws? They separate us and denigrate us. I tell you, we are not property. Nor is our blood unclean. And why are our priests not allowed to offer sacrifices?''

''I tell you,'' affirmed another, the best legal mind of her generation, ''in years to come this contract will work against us.''

The women were somber and read through the text again. As one woman, they confirmed all objections. The text would have to be revised. They called for Moses.

''Go back,'' they said, ''and tell God this Torah either dehumanizes us or leaves us out. For us this covenant is not righteous. For us, we deem it unacceptable.''

Once again Moses ascended Sinai and before God presented the petition of the women.

And God deliberated a long time upon the matter. Then God smiled and said to Moses, ''The women are righteous. They are correct and justified in demanding that the Law be revised. The time, however, is not yet right. Go down and tell the women to stand at the foot of the mountain.''

The women gathered at the foot of Mount Sinai. Suddenly, there rang out a voice from heaven—a *bat kol:*

''In the age of Blood and Fire and Clouds of Smoke, I will hear your plea. And because you will have waited all those thousands of years you shall know this. When you come before Me again, criticizing this Torah, asking that this Law be taught to you anew, I make you this promise. At that time, it will be your plea which will herald the age of the Messiah.''

Diane Levenberg

Deborah, wife of Lappidot, was a prophetess...and the Israelites would come to her for judgment....She summoned Barak, son of Abinoam [to fight Sisera]....[When he insisted that she accompany him, she said,] "...there will be no glory for you in that....God will deliver Sisera into a woman's hand." (Judges 4:4-9)

Why did Deborah become a pacifist?

Deborah sat hidden under a palm tree hoping that no one would see her. Her last case had exhausted her patience. She had spent the entire morning trying to convince a soldier who had killed a prisoner of war that he had sinned.

"Why?" he had demanded. "You said that Yael was the most blessed of women. And for what? For striking Sisera, crushing his head, smashing and piercing his temple with the tent pin when he was at her mercy. So what's wrong with what I did?"

Finally she had ordered him to bring a sacrifice and atone for his crime.

As the soldier left, he spat on the ground and said to the

81

crowd gathered outside, "Deborah's become a pacifist."

It was inconceivable that Deborah, who had once proudly led the people of Israel into battle, would condemn soldiers for killing prisoners of war. Yet she had done precisely that. At first, the elders ignored these decisions and continued to refer to her as a conqueress. Yael, however, knew the truth and avoided Deborah. Yael was still proud of the bloody act which had won her fame in Israel. Her answer to Deborah was to declare in public that Deborah had turned into an "old woman."

I was young once! To think that Barak and I were equals —at least at first, when he wouldn't do a thing without consulting me. He said, "If you will go with me, I will go; if not, I will not go." (4:8) But he changed after our victory. Though he went reluctantly into battle, he quickly forgot who had dragged him to glory once he gained manhood under fire. He sang my song too well. I struck up the chant and Barak dealt with the captives and the division of booty. Later it became his song—and hers! For Yael decided to become a woman warrior. Did she think she was imitating me?

Deborah knew she would never go to battle again, not even if Barak called. Barak had been irresolute about the necessity of war, but success had changed him and soldiering today was his major preoccupation. Now Deborah was the reluctant one. She had appropriated Barak's former uncertainty and translated it into sensitivity about wasting human life. Deborah now had a cause: she was determined never again to be responsible for shedding blood.

This type of thinking did not endear her to tribal leaders, who educated their troops to exteriorize evil and project it onto the enemy. Yael the warrior accepted their view. In becoming one of them, she denied her womanly, life-sustaining instincts and substituted manly acts of destruction.

Lately Deborah had felt that she was regarded as an alien. She heard mumblings that it was unnatural for women to be leaders. Am I getting old? Thinking back, she realized that a scurrilous smear campaign had begun on the anniversary of her return from the war. During one of the festivals celebrated by the people at Shiloh to commemorate their victory she had gone with a peace offering. Standing at the door of the Tent of Assembly was a self-appointed zealot who refused to allow her into the sanctuary, saying, "Woe unto the generation whose leader is a woman."

She had answered, "When it suited you, you created legends about me. You said I was like a hind let loose to conquer Sisera and that I sang goodly words in *my* song of victory. Now you are making puns about my name. 'Hornet,' you call me."

There was no bite in Deborah's alleged sting. She had become convinced it was not right for women to lead men into battle; moreover, it was wrong to build a society that required men to waste their lives and talents leading others into battle.

If Yael sets the tone for women, who will be left to point out the wasteful and destructive side of war?

Deborah's convictions did not sit well with the elders, and they denounced her as an illegitimate prophet. Sitting under her palm tree in the heat of the day, Deborah wondered whether history would treat her kindly. Will they write me out, as they did my ancestor, Miriam? Or will they tell posterity that I thought war was wrong, that it was a sin to revere combat and that I learned the hard way that our enemies' blood was also red?

* * *

"So may all your enemies perish, O Lord!
But those who love you shall be as the sun when
    it rises in its strength!

And the land was tranquil forty years."
                        (Judges 6:31)

Naomi Graetz

If a man would give all the substance of his house for love,
he would utterly be scorned. (Song of Songs 8:7)

What did Solomon have in mind when he wrote these words?

He stood at the window, gazing out to the fields and hills
below. The restlessness and brooding he had felt in the last
few months rose up again. He could feel the heat rise within
him. He knew he had everything he ever dreamed of: power,
a palace, the Temple he built to last forever in Jerusalem.
Why the discontent? King of Israel, he should be at peace.
He couldn't remember the last time he had not gotten what
he wanted.

A movement in the garden turned his head. It was a
servant passing through the corner where the Shulamite used
to stand for hours. Every woman but she was more than
willing to love and please him. Her continued refusals had
galled him to outrage. He had tried everything, the riches
of the palace, fine jewelry and garments—even the other
wives had both mocked and tried to persuade her. Stubborn
woman, and what for? A shepherd with a future no different
from his past. She wouldn't budge.

85

Solomon could have forced her, and many times his anger brought him close. How dare she spurn his ardor and passion! Her beauty was so different from all his other wives that when the palace guards had brought her to him, he almost had dismissed her outright. It was her lack of awe and interest in him and his palace which had fanned the flames of desire for her. No other wife could satisfy him. This Shulamite had turned the palace and his life into tumult. No peace existed while Solomon's desire was denied. More maddening was the quiet strength in her daily refusals, speaking only of her shepherd, while he, Solomon, King of Israel, offered her anything to be his.

The afternoon shadows grew longer. Solomon thought back to the day he had sent her home. She hadn't fallen all over him in gratitude (as he was used to from all the others). He had received no "thank you" for the freedom he had granted her. She had looked at him silently, knowingly, with eyes that saw right into his soul. Only prophets ever looked at him that way—certainly not any woman who had been given the privilege of his company.

That memory kept him at the window while the Sabbath hours flew by. She had rejected it all for the love of a shepherd. How absurd! Suddenly, Solomon realized he was jealous. His wives all adored him, or at least they pretended to. What if he were that shepherd? Would they have cast a second look at him? He knew the answer. In an instant he yearned to be that shepherd, the beloved of the Shulamite, to know that her devotion was for him, Solomon. He understood for the first time that he wanted to feel and give that deep, pure love to her, not only receive it. He ached for that bond he had never known and never would know. Yet...he had known a similar bond, before he had let the throne distance himself from his faith and devotion to God.

"Oh, God," he thought. "I've built a great temple to

honor You forever. I've made brilliant judgments which have gained me respect and admiration...but only through the eyes of the Shulamite do I realize how dreadful the distance has grown between myself and any other human being. How much greater the distance between myself and You, Adonai."

Tears began to flow. Solomon mourned his loss. He wept not out of anger and frustration, but out of grief for himself and what he had become.

The horns sounded the dinner hour. Solomon turned away from the window. A song could be written...perhaps to remember her, to remember the fierce, unshakeable love that she had for her shepherd. And when it is sung...I'll close my eyes and pretend I am that shepherd and she is my beloved. The peace of the Sabbath finally came over Solomon as it had not done in months.

"I am my beloved's and my beloved is mine." (Song of Songs 6:3)

Charlene Stern

20

"*Do not call me Naomi....Call me Marah, for the Almighty has made it very bitter for me.*" *(Ruth 1:20)*

Why does Naomi feel embittered, and how does this fit with the portrayal of Naomi in the remainder of the story?

Tomorrow was the day they were to return to Judah, and Naomi tossed as she tried to sleep. It wasn't just the anticipation of the trip that kept her awake, but her concern over the fate of her two daughters-in-law, Ruth and Orpah. They had been through so much together and had grown to love one another as though connected from birth. Ruth and Orpah had always respected Naomi's wisdom and sought her advice before they made any decisions, and now they were more devoted to her than ever.

Yet it was her love for them that led her to believe they should not return to Judah with her. As difficult as it would be for her to return without them, she was even more concerned about their future. She had no more sons to marry them, and she had no idea whether any other relatives would be in a position to marry them.

89

What is more, they would be foreigners there, and she could not predict how they would be treated. She recalled how frightened she had been as a child when, walking in the fields, she saw a woman insulted and mishandled by the men working there. She later learned the woman was a foreigner and assumed that must have been the reason she was mistreated. Until Naomi met Ruth and Orpah, she herself believed foreigners were "different." Ruth and Orpah had taught her otherwise.

Her thoughts came back to the decision about returning to Judah. Naomi felt reasonably certain that, out of respect for her, her friends and relatives would treat her daughters-in-law well, but what about the people who didn't know her and her family? And what if she became ill? Or died? The risk of taking her daughters-in-law back to Judah with her seemed too great, and Naomi was more convinced than ever that Ruth and Orpah must return to Moab.

Yet she sensed it would be a painful decision. Both daughters-in-law, and especially Ruth, had come to love the God of the Israelites and to be devoted to her people's way of life. What is more, Ruth had told Naomi about a dream in which the two of them were bound together, yet could move freely. What should she say if Ruth insisted on going with her?

Surely, Naomi thought, she didn't deserve such devotion —she, whose sins had brought sad days upon them all. Why would God take both of her sons if she were not a sinful woman? Surely it must have been her own failures that had brought about such catastrophes.

Her daughters-in-law saw her as no more responsible for their bad fortune than were they or anyone else. When she tried to speak to them of her guilt, they would laugh and attempt to reassure her. How could she be responsible, they would say, when she was the most generous, selfless person they knew. Such wonderful daughters-in-law they were. She could never do anything to bring harm upon them. No, they must return to Moab, and she—alone—to Judah.

Yet, what if it was God's will that Ruth return to Judah with her? If that were the case, she knew what she must do. She must make every effort to convince Ruth to return to Moab, but if Ruth insisted upon going to Judah with her, Naomi would accept it as God's will and not protest.

Making the decision was a relief, but Naomi still felt guilty and afraid. Suppose she did not deserve Ruth's devotion? Would she or her descendants be punished again? Naomi felt she must do something. She knew it might be considered superstitious, but she had been thinking about a change of name. The name "Naomi" suggested God's favor toward her, and surely that was presumptuous. She would ask to be called Marah, as a constant reminder of her bitter lot, and to assure a better future.

Marjory (Micki) Cort Seltzer

"If it please the king, let there go a royal commandment from him, and let it be written among the laws of the Persians and the Medes that it be not altered, that Vashti come no more before King Ahasuerus, and let the king give her royal estate unto another that is better than she." (Esther 1:19)

Should the maligned Queen Vashti's refusal to obey the king's commandment indicate feminist thoughts about the condition of women in her society?

A beautiful sunset settles over the lush garden adjacent to the royal house of King Ahasuerus. Queen Vashti sits alone on a bench gazing at the tumbling waters of a nearby fountain. Tears come to her eyes as she must leave this place and face the unknown. She will never again experience the joys of luxury and power and the love of Ahasuerus, her husband, her king.

This handsome, powerful man who reigns over a glorious kingdom, reaching from India to Ethiopia, can be very kind and tender when they are alone and away from everyone else. She loves him and will miss lying in his arms. On the fateful night that he commanded her to come to him, she could not obey. He wanted to parade her in front of scores of drunken men just to express his vanity, to display her as he would a costly possession. Her beauty should be for him alone; being made a public spectacle was repulsive to her. He must have been drunk himself. If he truly loved her, as he so often professed, why would he want to embarrass her in this way? She was not a slave or concubine; she was his queen.

For those seven days she, too, had entertained the wives of the men he wanted to impress. She had done her part with those doting women who curried her favor to enhance their status and who envied her power and good looks. After such a trying week, she deserved some privacy, a rest from the pressures of public demands.

Ahasuerus did not try to understand her feelings! He knew that she loved him and wanted to please him. Once more, vanity consumed him, deafening him to her entreaties. Now he felt wronged and embarrassed in front of his subjects. For this he could not forgive Vashti. He listened to his chamberlains, men who resented her because of the little influence she had had. Vashti remembered the times when she pointed out their unwise counsel and the king listened. Now they have their revenge. "They have succeeded in banishing me."

She knows that soon a new queen will reign. Rumors are that Esther is the favorite. Esther has beauty, intelligence, and a kind soul, all attributes to make the king happy. Will Esther be able to reach him in ways that Vashti could not? Can the new queen convey that she is another human being, a helpmate in ruling the kingdom, not a toy or possession for display? Even though Vashti envies this young woman, she realizes that Esther is not to blame for her present circumstances.

Vashti prays that one day women will be free to choose between refusing or accepting the demands of men. She hopes that the new queen will want and be able to help make this a reality.

Rose Luttinger

Epilogue

The choicest first fruits of your land you shall bring to the house of the Eternal your God.... (Exodus 23:19)

Who plants the field yielding choice first fruits?

It was a dark, dank, dismal day. She stood looking at the open field ahead of her, musing about all the rubble that had accumulated from previous generations. "How much better," she thought, "to remove some of the debris, plow the field, and plant seeds that will bring forth new life." So many layers of rock and boulders had piled up over the years, that even the men did not come to plant in the field anymore.

She stood looking at the mess. Ruminating, she remembered last year when she had talked about her idea to plant the field. "Impossible!" she had been told. "The work is too heavy. This is a man's job!" She had felt hurt, stung by the words. "Still,"—she looked across the field again— "What if...?" Visions of new growth sprang into her head. She started to smile, turned around and walked slowly away.

The next day the sun broke through the clouds, warming the earth. She returned and stood looking out over the field ahead of her. Suddenly, out of the stillness, a quiet voice commanded in her thoughts, *"DO IT!"* She looked around apprehensively, thinking someone had joined her. No. No one was there. Then she relaxed, smiled, and knew that the voice was hers. She had just given herself permission to go ahead. She lifted her foot, kicked at a pile of rubble, and watched the rocks scatter. Delighted at the results, she bent, grabbed a rock, and tossed it out of the field. "I don't need you here anymore," she thought. "Go pile up somewhere else." Then she set to work vigorously: kicking, lifting, heaving, and tossing the rocks.

At sunset she stopped. She looked at the cleared ground and thought about tomorrow's freshly plowed earth and the seeds she would scatter in the fertile ground. She turned and again walked slowly away, this time with a lighter step. Now she was confident that she was equal to the task.

Irene Fine

Author's Note: Despite all the warnings, the "field" I was determined to sow was Jewish studies. My goodness, the fruit has been delicious!

Sources

Bin Gorion, Micha Joseph. *Mimekor Yisrael.* Bloomington, IN: Indiana University Press, 1976.

Cantor, Aviva. *The Jewish Woman: A Bibliography, 1900-1985.* Fresh Meadows, New York: Biblio Press, 1987.

Christ, Carol P. "Women's Liberation and The Liberation of God: An Essay in Story Theology." In *The Jewish Woman—New Perspectives,* edited by E. Koltun. New York: Schocken Books, 1976.

Elwell, Sue Levi. *The Jewish Women's Studies Guide, Second Edition.* New York: University Press of America and Biblio Press, 1987.

Fine, Irene. *Developing a Jewish Studies Program for Women: A Springboard to History.* Doctoral Dissertation. Ann Arbor: University Microfilms International, 1981.

Fine, Irene. *Educating the New Jewish Woman, A Dynamic Approach.* San Diego: Woman's Institute For Continuing Jewish Education, 1985.

Freedman, Rabbi Dr. H. and Maurice Simons, eds. *The Midrash Rabbah.* London: Soncino Press, 1977.

Gellman, Marc. "Partners." *Moment.* January-February, 1978. (*ed. note.* Only one of the many modern midrashim written by Gellman and found in the issues of *Moment.*)

Ginzberg, Louis. *The Legends of the Jews.* Philadelphia: The Jewish Publication Society of America, 1937.

Holtz, Barry, ed. *Back to the Sources: Reading the Classic Jewish Texts.* New York: Summit Books, 1984.

Leviant, Curt. *Masterpieces of Hebrew Literature.* New York: KTAV Publishing House, Inc., 1969.

Patai, Raphael. *Gates to the Old City.* New York: Avon Books, 1980.

Plaskow, Judith. "Standing Again At Sinai: Jewish Memory From A Feminist Perspective." *Tikkun,* Vol. 1, No. 2.

Schwartz, Howard. *Gates to the New City.* New York: Avon Books, 1983.

Strack, Herman L. *Introduction to the Talmud and Midrash.* New York: Atheneum, 1978.

Weissler, Chava. "The Religion of Traditional Ashkenazic Women: Some Methodological Issues." *American Jewish Studies Review,* Vol. 12, No. 1.

Zones, Jane Sprague, ed. *San Diego Women's Haggadah, Second Edition.* San Diego: Woman's Institute For Continuing Jewish Education, 1986.

Readers

Rabbi Lenore Bohm, who edited as well as read these midrashim, is the spiritual leader of Temple Solel in North San Diego County. She is consultant to the Woman's Institute For Continuing Jewish Education and mother of a young son, David.

Irene Fine, contributor as well as reader, is Director of Jewish Studies at the Woman's Institute For Continuing Jewish Education. She is the author of *Educating the New Jewish Woman; Midlife, A Rite of Passage;* and *The Wise Woman, A Celebration*. Her family has recently increased to include her daughter-in-law, Kelly.

Elizabeth Resnick Levine, who also edited as well as read these midrashin, is a free-lance writer and editor, with an M.A. in Jewish Studies from Hebrew Union College— Jewish Institute of Religion. She lives in San Diego with her husband, Andrew Resnick, and two charming dogs, Goniff and Kugel.

Jane Sprague Zones, the book's editor, is a San Francisco-based medical sociologist whose major interests are health policy and women's health. She helped edit the *San Diego Women's Haggadah*. She is well-supported by her family: Stacey, Milo, and Isaac.

Contributors

Penina V. Adelman is a writer and social worker living in Massachusetts with her husband and son. She is the author of *Miriam's Well: Rituals for Jewish Women Around the Year* (Biblio Press).

Margot Azen holds a B.A. from Princeton and is a writer and playwright. She is co-editor of an anthology on Jewish feminist spirituality and is currently writing a feminist play.

Bonnie Feinman is co-founder of the Woman's Institute For Continuing Jewish Education, past San Diego area Director of the American Jewish Committee, and presently professionally active in the areas of human relations and youth services.

Randee Friedman is a Jewish music resource specialist. She is the anthologist of the recording *Sounds of Creation: Genesis in Song,* which offers a contemporary song to accompany each Torah portion in Genesis. Randee also teaches Torah cantillation and Jewish holiday celebration classes.

Helen Gotkowitz is a free-lance writer and active in the family business. Her background is in social work and teaching. She is the mother of four daughters and the wife of Joseph Gotkowitz.

Rabbi Lynn Gottlieb, spiritual leader of Nahalat Shalom in Albuquerque, is a master storyteller and ceremonialist. Since 1973 she has been teaching and inspiring audiences in the U.S., Canada, Europe, and Israel.

Naomi Graetz, a native New Yorker, made aliyah in 1967 and is on the faculty of Ben Gurion University in the Negev. She is chairperson of the Negev Branch of the Israel Woman's Network. Her aggadot have been published in the *Journal of Reform Judaism, The Jewish Spectator, The Melton Journal, Response,* and the *Jerusalem Post.*

Susan Gross, a former journalist, is interested in reading and writing modern feminist midrash. A native of Los Angeles, she now lives in Shreveport, Louisiana, with her husband and two young daughters.

Barbara D. Holender is the author of *Shiva Poems* (Andrew Mountain Press, 1986). Her book of midrash in poetry, *Ladies in Genesis,* is in search of a publisher.

Sylvia Karzen, recently retired after sixteen years with Jewish Family Services of San Diego, is spending her time writing, reading, traveling, and working on arts and crafts projects. She also spends time enjoying her three adult children and her two grandchildren, ages eight and four.

Diane Levenberg is the author of *Out of the Desert* (Doubleday, 1980). She is Associate Professor of English at Kutztown University in Pennsylvania.

Rose Luttinger is a 49-year-old part-time homemaker, part-time secretary who is in the midst of searching for new directions. Her midrash is her first attempt at writing.

Roxane Neal is co-founder and editor of the *Jewish Women's Newsletter.* She was an organizer of the 1983 Jewish Feminist Conference in Berkeley and is currently part of a woman's Torah study group and a Rosh Chodesh group.

Judith Plaskow, Associate Professor of Religious Studies at Manhattan College, has been writing, teaching, and speaking about feminist theology for almost twenty years. The ideas for the Lilith myth emerged from a Biblical/theological subgroup at the Grailville conference in 1972. Other members of the group were Karen Bloomquist, Margaret Early, and Elizabeth Farians.

Rayzel Robinson is Executive Director of Hillel at York University. She has an M.A. in Jewish Studies from Brandeis University and is a writer and songwriter currently at work on an anthology of Jewish feminist spirituality.

Faith Rogow is a Ph.D. candidate in women's and Jewish history at State University of New York, Binghamton. She is a composer of Jewish feminist music and has been an educator in the Jewish community for fifteen years.

Arlene Saidman is currently the librarian for Congregation Beth Israel in San Diego, as well as their curriculum coordinator for Judaic Studies. She has just co-authored a new Shiva Service called *Remembrance.*

Marjory (Micki) Cort Seltzer is managing editor of *Theory Into Practice,* an education journal (Ohio State University). She is married and has three children. Her women's group, whose discussion stimulated the writing of midrash, has used *Taking The Fruit* as a focus for discussion at summer services at Congregation Beth Tikvah.

Rabbi Ruth H. Sohn is a B'nai B'rith Hillel rabbi at Boston University. She lives with her husband and four-year-old daughter in Brookline and is a lover of midrashim, both traditional and modern.

Charlene Yetta Stern, a child of survivors, lives in Berkeley, California, with her husband and their three children. She is one of the founders of Congregation Beth El's twelve-year-old weekly Torah study group, to whom she first read her midrash aloud. She recommends you also read these out loud.

Esther K. Ticktin was born in Vienna, Austria, and came to the United States with her family in 1940. She is married and has three daughters and eight grandchildren. She is a practicing psychotherapist in Washington, D.C., and a member of the Fabrangen Havurah.

Ellen M. Umansky is Associate Professor of Religion at Emory University. The author of numerous articles on women and Judaism, as well as two books on Lily Montagu, founder of the Liberal Jewish movement in England, she is currently working on a book on spiritual healing and American Jews.

Your Own Midrash

Taking the Fruit: Modern Women's Tales of the Bible

Your Own Midrash

Taking the Fruit: Modern Women's Tales of the Bible

Your Own Midrash

Taking the Fruit: Modern Women's Tales of the Bible

Your Own Midrash

Taking the Fruit: Modern Women's Tales of the Bible

Your Own Midrash

Taking the Fruit: Modern Women's Tales of the Bible

Your Own Midrash

T35